SEA SHELLS

SEA
SHELLS

BY RUTH H. DUDLEY

Illustrated by Phoebe Erickson

THOMAS Y. CROWELL COMPANY

NEW YORK

34937
4/6/60

The author wishes to express her thanks to Dr.
Howard R. Hill, Curator of Zoology, Los Angeles
County Museum, Los Angeles, California, for his kind
help in editing this book.

The illustrator wishes to thank Mr. and Mrs. John
Wells of New Milford, Connecticut, for their kindness
in allowing the use of their shell collection.

To

Mother, with whom I first began gathering shells when I was small, indeed; to Violet Biscoe, my companion of many pleasant hours on our beautiful beaches; and to Jerry Garth, who guided us in the proper ways of a true conchologist. And, of course, to all my fine young friends and the new friends I hope to have when they read this book.

CONTENTS

SEA SHELLS

I THE LIMPET KNOWS ITS WAY HOME

We all have heard stories of dogs and cats that have found their way home, sometimes across a whole country. And this uncanny ability seems quite wonderful.

But even more startling is the fact that little sea animals have this instinct, too. True, they may

1

not travel so far—but they often go quite a distance. And they come back to the very spot they left.

These little sea animals are limpets. They are quite small, their shells being from one to two inches long. Some are a bit larger and measure as much as four inches.

Limpets are mollusks. The term *mollusk*, meaning "soft animal," refers to the bodies of a rather large group of creatures. Each has a body that is soft, boneless, and usually, though not always, protected by a shell.

The limpet's body consists of a foot, a mouth, and two feelers. And since the limpets have only one shell they are called univalves. Some species, the "seaweed limpets" for instance, make sea plants and grasses their home. They attach themselves to strong bits of seaweed and sway gently

Limpets attached to seaweed

back and forth with the movement of the sea.
Most limpets, however, live on rocks. Sometimes the whole surface of a rock will be covered

3

with these limpets. Yet each little limpet seems to have its own special spot. Very rarely are the true limpets found clinging to one another, although hundreds or thousands may be grouped on an area of only a few square feet.

The limpet fastens himself to the rock in such a way that his body is hidden beneath the shell and protected by it. The middle muscular part of his body is called the foot and he holds onto the rock with this. Very firmly, too. There he stays when he wants to rest, enjoying the spray from the sea.

When the limpet gets hungry he sticks out his foot, lifts up his shell and moves away from his special rock home. He can go quite rapidly, too, considering his size. He manages this motion by creating and releasing a vacuum in the many tiny tubes on the undersurface of his foot.

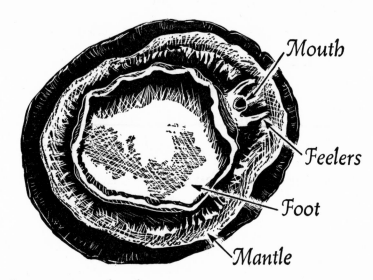

Mouth

Feelers

Foot

Mantle

Limpet upside down

In the limpet's mouth is a rather hard ribbon or bandlike affair with tiny teeth so small you really need a magnifier to see them. But this file-like ribbon, called the radula, is what he uses to scrape his food from the rocks. Seaweed or small bits of algae or vegetable matter found growing on rocks is what he generally eats.

Sometimes the limpet has to go quite a long

way from his home before he finds enough food to fill him. He often visits a great many different rocks and goes in many different directions. You might think that he surely must be lost—that he never could find his way back.

But always, without fail, when he has had enough to eat and is ready to turn back, he can find his way—not only to his own home rock but to his own exact spot on this rock. In fact, the limpet spends so much time in this same spot that quite often he leaves a mark or scar that is the same shape as his body and seems to be peculiarly his. And even though there may be hundreds of other limpets living on this same rock, and all of them going away for their food and returning, each one is able to come back to his very own spot. They never seem to get mixed up a bit.

6

Limpets on rock

It is almost impossible to push a limpet off his chosen place once he is fastened firmly to it. Small as he is—his area at the base is only one inch—he can cling so firmly with his foot, with those vacuum suckers of his, that it takes about a seventy-pound pull to remove him. This accounts for that saying, "sticks like a limpet!"

Limpets live several years—some up to ten. There are many kinds of limpets on both the east and west coasts of the United States. Some like the cold waters of both coasts, so you will find them in the northern sections. Others like the warm waters and live in the warmer sections such as southern Florida or southern California. Usually they are bowl shaped or cone shaped and rather small in size. One species found on the Mexican coast is larger than any we have in our oceans. It is large enough, in fact, to be used for a wash basin.

The largest one found on our west coast, the owl limpet, has a very handsome shell, three to four inches long, two to three inches wide. It is quite pretty outside, with olive brown mottling. But it is the inside of the shell—dark with a bluish white center, often marked with brown—that

8

Owl limpet

attracts the eye. Here, where the animal once lived, lovely markings show the outline of an owl sitting on its perch.

The tortoise-shell limpet, a cold water mollusk common on the Maine and Alaskan coasts, is smaller but has owl-shaped markings on the inside, too. Outside it is very lovely with brown and green stripes and circles of black and white.

9

An interesting smaller species—about one inch long, that lives in southern Florida—has gray or buff sides with fine black rays running across it.

One species of limpet, found on both the east and west coast, is called the "keyhole" limpet—because it has a hole at the top shaped very much like a keyhole.

There are many other kinds of limpets and

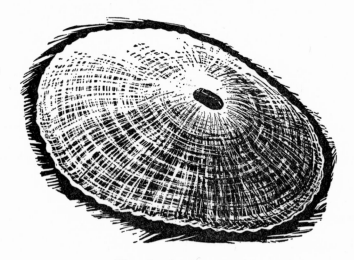

Keyhole limpet

each one very interesting in its own special way. It is fun to hunt along the beaches for limpet shells and to see how many different kinds can be found. An especially good time to do this is after there has been a storm at sea or there have been some very high tides.

When looking for live limpets, go down when the tide is low and search among the seaweed, the rocks, and the tidal pools. Since most limpets make their home near shore, they are left high and dry at this time.

Colors of the limpets blend in with the colors all around them so they are not too easy to see. And since their shells are often partly covered with brownish sea growths, they are very nicely camouflaged.

However, if you look carefully you will find them, often on the underside of rocks where the

11

waves will not smash against them too roughly or where their enemies, such as sea gulls and crabs, will not too easily spy them.

In order to breathe, limpets must lift their shells slightly. This means they cling rather loosely to their home spot when undisturbed. But at the slightest hint of danger they fasten themselves so tightly it's almost impossible to push them off without breaking the shell.

So come quietly if you wish to get them off whole. Slip a broad-bladed knife under one quickly and it will roll off in your hand. This way you can study the animal inside—the strong muscular foot, the two feelers, and the interesting mouth.

For the limpet is, indeed, a fascinating mollusk. And its little shell home is a lovely one—quite important in anyone's collection.

II "OLIVES" IN THE SAND

Olives can be found in the sand as well as on the grocer's shelf. But a different kind, of course. The olives found at the beach are shells. And they are called that because they look like the olive fruit.

These shells are smooth and small, oval in

13

shape, with deeply notched, long and narrow openings. They are more like a ripe olive in color since many of them are purple. But there are several different kinds. Some are almost white, others are dove colored with purple trimmings, some are gray or brown or yellow with quite a variation of lines and markings.

In fact, one of the interesting things about these olive shells is their very wide range in design and color. In a handful of the same species very few will be colored or marked alike.

You could say, too, that these olive shells are stuffed because a very curious creature lives inside. This little animal likes to dig down in the sand just far enough so his shell is covered. He does this digging with a little plow-shaped foot which is very quick. In no time at all he can whisk himself out of sight.

14

He doesn't like to be out in the air if he can help it. Nor does he like to be alone. He is happiest when he is living just under the surface of the sand with his friends and family.

But he doesn't stay long in one spot. He is quite active, always scurrying around and on the move. You might dig down in the sand at low tide sometime and find a large group of these fellows. But if you came back just a short while later, they might all be gone.

Although the olive loves to lie buried in the sand, he has to have water for his gills—much as a fish needs water to live, or as we need air for our lungs. He has a very convenient arrangement which enables him to get this necessary water even while lying securely buried in the sand. He has a siphon, or little "pipe," which he sticks up through the sand into the clear water above. And

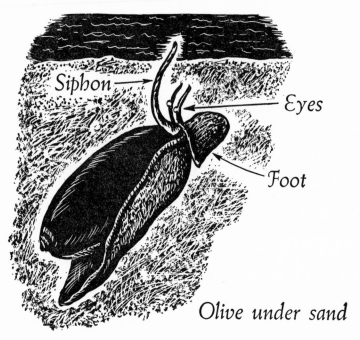

Siphon

Eyes

Foot

Olive under sand

he draws down all he needs through this siphon.

The smooth, polished texture of olive shells makes them delightful to hold. It is interesting to note, however, that these shells as a rule seem much prettier, more polished and smooth, when the animals are living in them. This is true of most sea shells, but especially of olive shells.

This is because of a neat covering the animal has for his shell. It consists of folds of soft, moist skin, called the mantle, which he spreads over his shell much of the time. He does this in order to protect the shell from injuries it might otherwise receive from being buffeted about. Empty shells, not having this protection, soon get rather scraped and worn. They lose their smooth shininess.

It isn't known for certain just how long all the different sea animals live. Generally the smaller animals do not live as long as the larger ones. The olive lives several years at least, as do most of the mollusks.

Olives like warm, tropical waters and you will find them in the southern waters of both our coasts. One species, called the "lettered olive," has a pattern of dark markings on its shell that looks like letters or hieroglyphics. This shell, about two inches long, can be found along the coast all the way from North Carolina, around Florida and to all the Gulf states. It is found also in the West Indies.

There is a larger species, about four inches long, found in the Gulf of California. It is called the tent olive, or camp olive, because the markings on its shell look like an encampment of tents.

Another pretty species, the netted olive, found in southern Florida, has a fine netlike pattern of purplish brown lines covering its pale whitish shell. It usually is about one and one-half inches in length.

There is a smaller group of olive shells, called the olivella, meaning "little olive," also found on both coasts. One kind, Say's olivella, is found from North Carolina to the West Indies. About one-half inch in length, it is very common in Florida, where it is often referred to as the "Panamas."

All California olives belong to this "little olive," or olivella, group. They are quite common on the beaches there. One interesting kind, the San Pedro rice shell, has a pretty shiny bluish or brown coloring, striped often with yellow.

If you're down by the shore and notice little pellets of sand being lifted up here and there, you can guess pretty surely that a group of these little fellows are buried there. It's as though they were peeking up every now and then to see what is going on in that strange world above.

Low tide is the best time to hunt these olive shells. Look along the mud flats, sandy beaches, in tide pools, and on seaweed for the various species. If you happen across an olive shell that is

19

scurrying along the rocks at a good rate you can be sure that the true olive mollusk isn't in that shell. The olive mollusk moves slowly. The shell probably has been taken over by a hermit crab. These hermit crabs make a practice of taking over shells which have lost their real owners, through accident or storm, and just move in. Since they have no shells of their own they depend on these empty shells of others for their protection.

The smooth, polished olive shells have been used and admired through the ages. Indians along both coasts were making them into necklaces and bracelets long before our forefathers arrived on these shores. And they used these olive shells also as wampum–a means of exchange–just as we use money. Evidence of this has been found among buried Indian relics.

Our own people have used these pretty shells,

20

too, through the years, to decorate their homes in various ways. By grinding off the apex, or tip, of the shells they were able to string them and make them into draperies, portieres, and the like.

People today like these shells too. And no wonder—they are so smooth, highly polished, and beautiful. You'll find them in all the coast town curio shops—and in many inland hobby shops too. And, of course, in any good shell collection!

III THE PECTEN CAN SWIM SWIFTLY

You've seen Overseas Ribbons and Purple Hearts of course. But chances are you've never seen anyone wearing a St. James shell. Long ago, in the middle ages, heroes did wear them, however.

If you'd been living in those days you'd have seen young men wearing them when they returned from a crusade. And they wore them proudly, too. People would stop to look at them. For it meant that they had been to the Holy Land. It meant that they were crusaders.

It all started, so the story goes, when a brave young hero on the First Crusade picked up a pretty shell he saw and stuck it gaily on his cloak. The other crusaders liked the idea. They decided to make this shell their badge. Later it became so popular and important that many orders of brave knights used its design on their coats of arms.

And this St. James Shell they used was very much like our own little scallop shell, or pecten. Perhaps you have found one, if you've ever been to the beach. It is easy to recognize by its "ears" which stick out on either side at the top. Some kinds have only one "ear," but in most you will find two.

23

It is a very beautiful shell. So it is no wonder that the knights liked it. The pecten is a bivalve. That is, it has two shells, hinged at the top. It is brightly colored in shades varying from dark red, light orange, and yellow to reddish brown. Sometimes you will find a very rosy pink one. And again you might find one that is almost white.

The animal that lives in this pecten shell is very

Pecten shell open, showing eyes on the two edges of the mantle

"smart." In fact, next to the octopus, the scallop is considered the "cleverest" of all mollusks—if we can think of mollusks in that way. It has a row of shining "eyes" along the edge of its mantle or skin. And these eyes quickly warn it of danger. It then darts away by clapping the two parts of its shell together. It can swim quite swiftly through the water just by flapping these shells.

Two jets of water are driven out through the openings in the mantle by the sudden clapping of the shells. This furnishes the power that drives the pecten so rapidly through the water. Since its shells are generally much thinner and less able to protect it than those of many of our mollusks, it needs this fast action to get away from its enemies—such as crabs, fish, and the like.

Sometimes a pecten will dive right into the mud when it is being chased. Then it will quickly clap its shells and make the water all around it so muddy that its enemy can't find it.

The pecten likes to swim around in the water. But it likes to rest sometimes, too. Especially when there's a storm at sea and the water is rough, it likes to be in a safe and quiet spot. So it finds a strong seaweed and climbs on it. Then, very cleverly, so it won't fall off, the pecten fastens itself to the weed.

There is a little notch in the back shell just under the left "ear." And through this notch the pecten sticks out a sort of finger and spins some threads. In this way he can fasten himself to the seaweed and sleep quietly and safely until he wants to untie himself and go for a swim again.

Some pectens are quite large, around six or seven inches across. Others are very tiny, no bigger than a dime. Pectens are found in every ocean in the world. Some are cold-water mollusks and so like to live in northern waters—often out where it is very deep.

One such species, called the deep-sea, or giant, scallop, gets to be seven inches across and is the largest American scallop. It is called the commercial species because it is used for food. It is found from Newfoundland to New Jersey. The Iceland scallop is another one liking the cold. He lives in the seas from Iceland to Maine, as well as in northern Europe.

Still other pectens like to live where the waters are warm. The calico scallop is one of the commonest on our southeastern beaches. There all kinds of shell novelties are made from these pretty shells. As its name implies, it has quite a variety of color combinations and patterns, showing white, purple, orange, yellow, brown, rose, and so on. It gets to be one and one-half inches long and is found from North Carolina to Cuba. A close relative of this calico scallop (about two inches long) is found from Florida along the Gulf coast to Texas. One of its shells is usually mottled black and white and the other shell is pure white with sometimes a tint of yellow.

The west coast has its pectens, or scallop shells, too, in both the cold and warmer regions. One

Calico pecten

Broad-eared
pecten

species has been dredged even from the icy waters off Alaska and in the Bering Sea.

In southern California an interesting species, the broad-eared scallop, has a small fragile shell with a diameter of one inch. And its unequal ears are nearly as broad as its shell.

The purple-hinged scallop is another interesting California species. When young it's a pretty little fan-shaped shell like the other pectens. It swims and plays around in the water just like all its relatives. But when it gets to be about an inch long a change takes place. First a purplish spot appears up near the hinge, on the inside of the shells. And soon after this it stops playing around, attaches itself to some fixed object, such as another shell or a rock, and stays there for the rest of its life.

It keeps on growing, even though fastened down. But instead of growing evenly and symmetrically as other, unattached pectens do, it grows in whatever direction there is the most room. And often these pectens get themselves into rather strange shapes. Soon the shells begin to thicken, the pretty colors fade, and much of the pecten prettiness is lost.

Dead specimens of these strange shells are often found washed up along the California beaches. And two interesting things can be seen in every one found. The purplish spot near the hinge still remains bright as ever—though grown larger with the years. And, also at the hinge, the distinct outline of the young pecten can clearly be seen, just as it looked when it fastened itself down and before it took on the new, distorted growth.

A few pectens, such as the bay scallop of the eastern coast, live in shallow water and are common among the eel grass. But since most pectens like to live in deeper water, you probably won't find any whole shells when you go hunting them at the beach.

Many lovely single pecten shells can be found, however, washed up by the tides. And these will make beautiful additions to your collection. Especially if you try to get a wide variety of kinds, sizes, and color combinations.

IV THE MUSSEL IS A SPINNER

A storm at sea may be mighty interesting to watch. Great waves smashing fiercely against a rocky shore line, frothing and fuming, flinging white spray high into the air. Beautiful to see, all this—when you're safe on dry land!

If you were out there, instead, in a frail boat

it could be mighty dangerous. Just as it is for the fragile sea shells. That's why, after a storm, you can find so many shells and sea animals washed up on the beach. It was just too rough for the smaller or more delicate ones to survive.

But there are some sea animals that seem to love the wildly smashing waves. None of the quiet, calm safety of the ocean floor for them. Nor the more sheltered nooks and crannies where other sea creatures often hide. They choose, instead, the broad open face of the rocks; the full pounding force of the waves. And they do seem actually to enjoy it.

These bold creatures are a common type of shell animal known and found the world over— the mussels. If you've ever been to the beach you may have seen them attached to the rocks along the shore line.

33

Mussel spinning byssal hairs

The mussel, like the pecten, is a bivalve. That is, its shell is made up of two sides, hinged together. And it builds its home upon rocks—firmly and securely like the wise man in the Bible.

When it is very tiny and young it is sent out into the ocean to care for itself. If it stayed in the water, just swimming around, it surely would not survive. Fortunately some instinct sends it to the firm ocean rocks. Here it picks out a nice open spot and decides to settle down—usually for life (which is around ten years).

Somehow this young mussel seems to know that he must fasten himself down if he wants to stay there—and in a hurry, too—before the tide comes sweeping in and the waves dash him off.

How does he do it? With threads—a special very strong, horny kind which he has the power to spin. These tough sets of threads are called byssuses, or byssal hairs. And they are pushed out by a gland in his foot.

This foot of his doesn't amount to much in some ways. It's a narrow foot, soft and weak. It can't be used to dig with as can the olive's foot, for instance. Nor can the mussel go walking around on it the way the limpet walks with his. But it does have a very important function—that of spinning these threads.

35

There's a little gland in the mussel's foot which sends out a sticky kind of substance, rather like our liquid glue. And this hardens almost as soon as it meets the air. So when the young mussel wants to fasten himself down to his rock home, he holds his foot against the rock surface and sends out this sticky substance. The stickiness immediately hardens against the rock, forming a strong, horny thread. Drawing his foot in slowly, he spins more and more threads until he is very firmly attached to his home. So firmly, in fact, that it's a task to try to pull the shell loose.

Once fastened down he is ready for the tide when it comes booming in. Eager for it, in fact, because it brings him food and refreshment. He has only to open his shell to breathe in the salty foam which purifies his blood. And to catch in his mouth the tiny sea animals and plants, afloat

36

on the waves, which make a good meal for him.

Usually the mussel stays here on his firm rock home all his life. He doesn't even move about very much. Certainly he never goes swimming as the pecten does. Nor wandering all over the rocks as the limpet does.

Once in a while he'll change his position or

move to a new spot nearby—never very far. He does this by reaching his foot out as far as possible and spinning new threads. Then, bringing pressure to bear, he pulls the old anchoring threads loose, a few at a time—even yanking some out by the roots. Finally he draws himself forward by hauling in on the new byssal hairs and settles down in this new spot for a while. When he does move, it is very slow work. But this doesn't seem to bother the mussel. He seems quite content just taking life easy. Just lying on the rock and letting the waves wash over him and bring him food.

Mussels do not all live on rocks. Some fasten themselves to piers, wharves, or mud banks—anything handy so long as it's firm and solid. The main enemies of the mussel are man and the starfish.

Mussels are found on all the shores of the world. And so, of course, they are on both our Atlantic and Pacific coasts. Walk along the beach at low tide and you will be amazed to see great masses of these mussels attached to the rocks or along the exposed piers.

One species, the California mussel, is found on the west coast from Alaska to Mexico and is quite common along the surf-beaten rocks of the California coast. Its shells are purple, mixed with shadings of white and brown, and they sometimes grow as long as eight inches, but usually are smaller. The Indians of California sharpened these mussel shells to hard, cutting points and set them in the tips of their harpoons.

A smaller species, the hooked mussel, can be found from Chesapeake Bay to Florida and along the Gulf coast. It has thick shells with thin, crooked ridges and at the hinged end there is a beaklike hook. An inch or two in length, it is dark brown in color.

The blue mussel, or edible mussel, is found in masses all along the Atlantic coast as well as on the Pacific coast. Its smooth, regular shell is bluish black and about two or three inches long. It is often found, too, living in quiet waters.

There's a large family related to these seacoast mussels, called fresh-water mussels. They live in

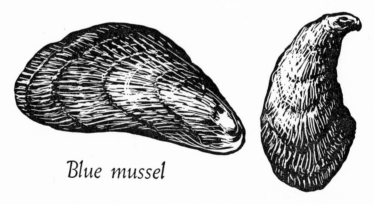

Blue mussel

Hooked mussel

the sandy, muddy, or gravelly bottoms of rivers and streams and in still water. There are many different species and one kind or another can be found throughout most of the United States.

Perhaps you live along a river and have seen them there. One species, the monkey-face, is common through the Mississippi drainage area south to the Tennessee and Arkansas rivers. Another, called the squaw-foot, is found on mud or sand bottoms in fairly deep, quiet water in the larger rivers from Ohio to Iowa.

The lady-finger, one of the most common of the fresh-water mussels, is found throughout the St. Lawrence and its tributaries, and through both the Mississippi and Alabama river systems.

There are so many different kinds of mussels you'll find it easy to add some of these to your collection, no matter where you live.

41

V THE PIDDOCK CARVES HIS HOME

If you wanted to drill a hole in a very hard rock you wouldn't think of using a shell. Not for a tough job like that.

But there is a sea animal that does this very thing. It uses its own shell for drilling into rock so hard that only a powerfully swung sledge hammer could break through to its burrow, or hole. This shell animal is the common piddock or rock clam.

The piddock is a bivalve—it has a shell which is divided into two separate parts, or valves, and hinged together. This shell is quite fragile and thin—though this is difficult to believe when you think of the hard rock it drills into.

Just how the piddock makes its home in this amazing way is still somewhat of a mystery. Some people who have studied the piddock's ways think the animal must have some secret means of making its hole in this hard rock. They think he may give out a chemical of some sort, which helps soften or wear away the stone. But they never yet have been able to find any evidence of this.

Most authorities agree that the work is done

by the piddock's shell and foot—work that takes a great deal of patience, effort, and stick-to-it-iveness.

To begin with, the young piddock, having spent a short childhood of freedom playing about in the sea, suddenly decides he would like a home to live in. He thinks it would be nice to settle down in peace and quiet—and in a good safe place.

So he looks around and finds a spot he likes, on some hard rock surface in deep water, for instance—much as we might pick out a lot on which to build a house. Then he sets to work. He starts the hole by grasping bits of sand in his foot and rubbing these against the surface of the rock.

This is not too easy a task as you well can imagine. But the piddock keeps at it until he has made an entrance roomy enough to get his shell part

44

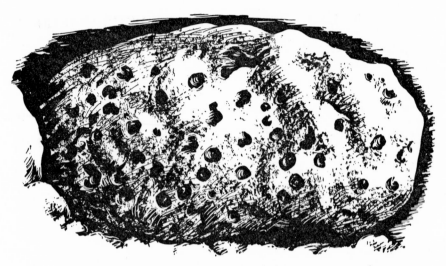

Holes bored by piddocks in a rock

way in. But this is only the beginning—the foundation of his home you might call it. There still is much work to be done.

The piddock next sticks his muscular foot on the hard rock surface. This foot grips the rock like a suction disk and holds the animal firmly. Then he twists and rocks himself on this foot and presses his shells outward so that they rub against

45

the entrance walls. His shells, though thin, are rough on the outer sides. Very slowly, by this constant rubbing, they grind off the inner rock wall.

This is slow, hard work, of course. But the piddock is building his permanent home where he will spend the rest of his life so it does take time and effort. Even when he finally has his little home made, however, he isn't entirely through. For the piddock is still young and growing. And as he grows he must keep making his house larger to make room for his bigger shell. Once inside his home he is there for life. He never leaves.

But he does rest quite a bit of the time now. He doesn't even have to go hunting for his meals, as the limpet must do, for instance. The piddock has long tubelike things, or siphons, which come in

Crab nipping at piddock's siphons

very handy. When he gets hungry or feels the need of oxygen he just sticks out these siphons and draws in all the food and air he wants. His food, like that of the mussel, consists of tiny sea animals and plants afloat on the water.

The piddock is quite safe from harm in his snug home, except that sometimes a starfish or crab will nip off the ends of his siphons if he's not quick enough about drawing them back in.

The shells of these rock-boring piddocks are

47

phosphorescent. If you could happen upon a rock filled with their holes on a dark night, when the water was moving around them, you'd be surprised to see a pale, weird light glowing up!

There are quite a few kinds of piddocks found in all the seas of the world, and their life span runs around eight to ten years—sometimes less, sometimes longer. Some piddocks dig in wood, some in clay and some deep down in sandy mud.

The rough piddock, grayish white and two to four inches long, is found on both the Atlantic and Pacific coasts. It likes to burrow in mud or hard clay.

One species, the common piddock, about two inches long, burrows in the rocks along the California and Oregon coasts. A common wood piddock, grayish white and one inch long, is found from New England to Florida. The best way to

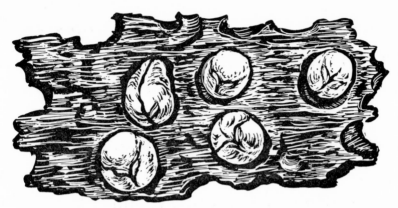

Piddocks burrowing into wood

find this species is to look in waterlogged timbers cast up on the beach. In fact, this piddock can sometimes be found on most any of our beaches in timber that has floated in from all over.

Another tiny species, called the little piddock, burrows into the hard shells of other mollusks, such as the abalone, and makes what is called a "blister pearl." This pearl is formed when the abalone, trying to keep the little piddock out, adds more and more layers of shell to the spot where

49

the piddock is burrowing. This causes a raised place on the shell, called a blister. It is very pretty with iridescent colors. It is removed and used, just as pearls are, in pins, brooches, and the like.

All piddock shells are pretty and fun to find. Since the shells are fragile and easily separated, single ones are more often found than are the double, or whole, shells. But even single ones are nice to have in your collection.

One species most sought after by shell collectors, and the loveliest of all piddocks, is the beautiful angel's wing. This shell is snowy white, six to eight inches long, and gracefully formed. The two parts of the thin and fragile shell touch only at one small point near the top. And when these parts are carefully spread open they look for all the world like the lovely pictures we have seen of an angel's wings.

This shell can be found from Cape Cod to the West Indies. It is most common in Florida, however, and is seen only occasionally north of Virginia.

If you find an angel's wing for your collection, you are lucky indeed. But you can always trade for one, of course.

VI THE COWRY LIKES TO HIDE

It seems unusual to think of a shell animal as being modest or shy. But the cowry, found mostly in the Pacific, is just that.

Strange, too, that it should be so because the cowry has one of the most beautiful shells imaginable. And the little animal that lives in it is lovely, too. It is very brightly colored and most graceful as it glides along over the rocks.

But the cowry doesn't like to be seen. It always tries to hide among the rocks and seems to hope that no one will spy it. Perhaps, since it is so beautiful, it has to hide so people won't pick it up.

Cowries have smooth, well-rounded shells that curve around to an opening. This opening is long and runs the full length of the shell. And it has little teeth like ridges along both edges.

Not only are the cowries beautifully colored but they have a layer of enamel over the whole shell. And this gives them a very bright, polished look. You would think someone had rubbed and rubbed them until they shone.

It's no wonder, then, that people like these shells and hunt for them whenever they can; not only here in America but in all parts of the world people like to have them. In the Fiji Islands the natives value them highly. It makes them seem quite important to wear a cowry shell. And the chiefs wear the shells as marks of royalty, much as some kings wear crowns.

In Borneo the tribes love to use cowry shells to decorate themselves. In India these shells trim the harnesses of horses and elephants. And all through Africa and the South Seas cowry shells have been used a great deal as money. So much so, in fact, that one kind actually is called the money cowry. Probably over there native boys and girls would rather have cowry shells than nickels—not only because of their great value to them, but because they love to shake the cowry shells and hold them to their ears to hear the "sea sounds." They think the sound of their native sea is imprisoned in the shells.

A strange thing about the cowry is that it seems to grow even more lovely as it gets older. It seems to have a wonderful power of painting and decorating its shell home in gay and bright designs—and with colors that grow prettier and prettier.

Along with this added beauty, the cowry shell grows larger, too. Authorities believe that two or three times during the life of the cowry (five to ten years or longer) it goes into hiding for a short time for the purpose of expanding and beautifying its shell home. While there the animal gives out an acid of some sort that slowly dissolves the inside of the shell as the outside of the shell is enlarged. In this way more room is made for its growing body and newer, brighter colors are added to its shell home, much as we might build onto and redecorate our homes.

One thing that keeps the cowry shell so shining

and clean is its covering, or mantle. As the animal crawls over the rocks or among the seaweed this reddish brown mantle folds up over it like an envelope, nearly covering the shell. It is like the olive in this respect. And, like the olive, the shell is much shinier when found with the animal in it. When empty and washed up on the beach it often has been tossed about by the waves so much that its glossiness has been worn away.

There are a great many kinds of cowries in the world—at least one hundred and fifty that we know about. But of all these, there are only three kinds found on the Atlantic coast of the United States. And only one on the California coast.

One kind of cowry found in fairly shallow water from North Carolina south (but mostly in Key West) is from four to six inches long and has such a very high polish you could actually use it as a mirror. The color of this shell is a light chestnut mixed with purple. And there are whitish spots all over the whole shell which seem fairly to shine beneath the enamel. Because of these spots it is called the measled cowry.

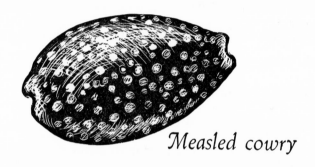

Measled cowry

The California cowry is very pretty, too. Up to two inches long, it is white along its opening but its back is a beautifully polished brown. Because of its coloring it is also called the nut brown cowry.

Since only four species live here in the United States, it may not be too easy for you to find specimens for your collection. However, cowries are so beautiful and so popular that thousands of all kinds are imported to our country every year. So it isn't difficult to find them for sale in most novelty or souvenir shops throughout the United States—even in many five-and-ten-cent stores.

If you have more of one kind than you want it's a good idea to trade around until you have a good, wide selection of these lovely cowries. No collection is complete without them.

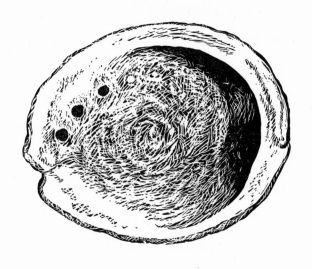

VII THE ABALONE HAS RAINBOW COLORS

If someone told you he had found a couple of "ears" while walking along the beach you might get quite excited.

That is, you might until you saw them. Then you would know, of course, that these "ears" had nothing to do with any part of a human body.

59

They would be "sea ears," a common name for the beautiful abalone shell—because it is shaped somewhat like a person's ear.

Like the limpet, the abalone is a univalve. That is, he has only one shell. Also like the limpet, the abalone fastens himself to a rock with his muscular foot so that his body is hidden beneath his shell and protected by it.

The abalone is much bigger than the limpet, however. Some are as wide as seven inches and as much as ten inches long. Most of the shells are smaller than this, though. The abalone is far handsomer than the limpet too—when you get to know him. He is so very handsome that often he is called the "rainbow shell." But you certainly might wonder why when you see the rough, dull color of his shell as he is clamped against a rock. If you ever have found an empty abalone shell

Abalone—outside of shell

washed up on the beach, however, you know the reason for this lovely name of his. It's the inside of the shell that is so beautiful. Every color of the rainbow can be seen in some of them—in the lovely green abalone, for instance.

And in the center of the shell there is a spot most colorful of all. It is the spot where the body was fastened tightly to the shell. If you ever have seen a peacock's tail, you will have some idea of the beautiful array of colors found in this particular spot on the inside of the abalone's shell. And you cannot help but admire the pearly, polished feel or texture of the shell's inside.

Because of its beauty and hard, polished surface the abalone shell is very much in demand for making pearl buttons, inlaid work, and for making trinkets, jewelry, and dishes of many kinds. Even the rough-looking outside of the shell is a lovely thing to see and feel after it has been cleaned and polished.

"Blister pearls" made by the abalone have bright, iridescent colors; are valued by collectors and souvenir hunters; and are often made into novelty jewelry. These pearls are formed when a tiny rock or a coarse grain of sand gets wedged inside the shell and bothers the animal. Since he has no way to get it out, he just grows a few extra layers of pearly shell and covers it over so it won't bother him any more.

This causes the very pretty raised spot called the blister pearl. Sometimes another smaller sea animal, such as the little piddock, bores into its shell and the abalone forms one of these blisters to keep it out.

Because the abalone is so beautiful and useful —he is used for food, too–people often go hunting him. Divers have special equipment to go down among the rocks at the bottom of the sea in search of the abalone.

So, of course, the abalone tries to keep out of the way as much as he can. He fastens himself beneath overhanging rocks and in crevices and depressions where he will not so easily be seen. And he hangs on with all his might when he hears an

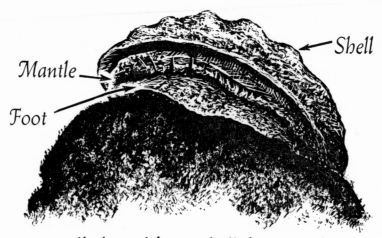

Abalone lifting shell from rock

enemy coming. So tightly, in fact, that we humans must use an instrument of some kind, such as a broad-bladed knife, to get him off.

The abalone's food is vegetable matter—sea lettuce, kelp, and the like—which he gets from the rocks where he lives. And he has a very handy gadget with which to get it, too—his tongue. It's not an ordinary tongue however. The abalone's tongue, flat and about as long as your finger, is

64

covered with sharp little teeth. When he is hungry he just sticks out his tongue, scrapes his dinner off the rocks, and brings it in, shredded fine and ready for swallowing.

The abalone has two eyes which stick out from his head on short stalks. He also has two long tentacles and a broad, central snout, at the end of which is a tiny hole of a mouth. When he wants to go walking he lifts up his shell, sticks out his head, and goes walking along on the undersurface of his body, or foot. He goes at a pretty good gait, too, for having to carry such a heavy shell. But when the abalone wants to stay put he can fasten himself very tightly to his rock home with that powerful grip of his.

The abalone has a row of holes near one edge of his shell. Perhaps you can see them in the illustration. These holes act as a sort of ventilator for him so he can always keep clean, and they enable him to breathe even when clamped tightly against a rock. The limpet, not having these convenient holes, must lift its shell slightly in order to breathe.

The abalone uses these holes in still another way. His foot, or main part of the body, has a rim of black skin and above this a black mantle fringed with tiny feelers about one inch long. He thrusts these feelers out through the holes and is able to sense with them the presence of enemies, such as sea birds, and the location of food.

The abalone doesn't have these holes in his shell when he is a baby. He's probably too young to know how to use them properly. But as his shell gets larger a row of holes appears along its edge. And new holes keep opening up as the shell grows. Then, since he does not need too many, the abalone closes up the old ones with a hard

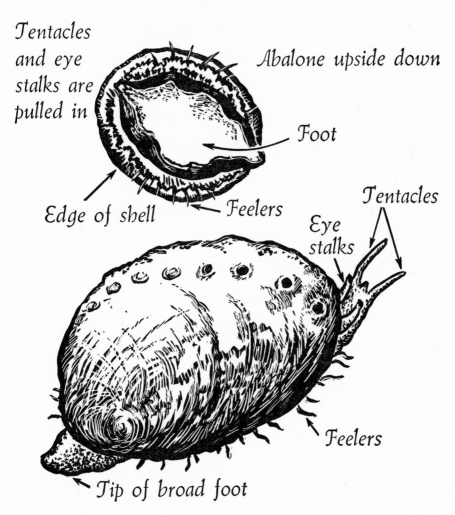

Tentacles and eye stalks are pulled in

Abalone upside down

Foot

Edge of shell

Feelers

Tentacles

Eye stalks

Feelers

Tip of broad foot

Abalone in his shell

substance he manufactures inside his shell. That way only a certain number stay open at any one time. If you look closely at the illustration you can see where the old holes have been closed up. Just how long the abalone lives is not definitely known—at least thirteen years, probably longer.

If your home is on the east coast of the United States, you will not be able to find any abalone shells when you go to the beach. But there are plenty of them on the west coast. Some abalones are found as far north as Oregon but most live in the warmer waters of California. In fact they are usually thought of as the most typical shell of California and they play quite an important part in the industry of that state where all parts of the animal are used.

The abalone also is found in Japan, Africa, Australia, and a few smaller ones in the Mediterranean and along the coast of England. But none are found in the West Indies.

It always is exciting to find one of these beautiful shells as you probably know if you live near any of these places or have ever visited them and gone hunting for shells. After a storm at sea the California beaches often are strewn with lovely specimens of these shells. You can find them in all sizes from beautiful tiny ones less than an inch long to really big ones, and in various colors, too —red, green, purple, or black. It's a fine time then to get a good selection.

If you do not have an opportunity to find any abalones and would like to have some for your collection you might write to a pen pal about making a trade. You will probably have some kinds of shells that he doesn't have.

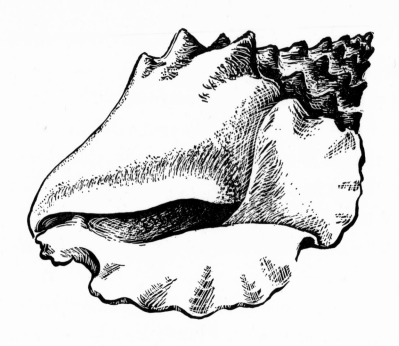

VIII THE CONCH CAN LEAP ABOUT

You have heard of Mexican jumping beans.
Perhaps you have had some at one time or another and watched in amazement. You may even
have tried to find out what made them act that
way.

There's a shell animal, too, that does some strange jumping about—for a shell animal, that is. It's the conch. And he turns somersaults!

Just place him on his back and watch. There—over he goes in as neat a somersault as you'd wish to see. And he is quite a jumper, too. Especially when he is frightened. He has been known, even, to jump out of fishermen's boats—when the fishermen weren't looking.

The conch is an intelligent creature. He has two well-developed eyes that stand out on thick eye stalks. And he has a good sense of smell which directs him to his food—dead fish and such things. In fact, one way to catch him is to put out some meat in a spot where he is apt to be, and then just sit back and wait. Pretty soon he will smell the meat and come hurrying. However, if you try to catch him he will sense your presence from quite

71

a long way off, no matter how quietly you advance. And very likely he'll be off, with quick leaps and turns, back toward the water. He has a big, heavy shell to carry around and a stout body so his quickness is all the more remarkable.

His oddly shaped foot is what gives him this swiftness. It is very narrow in front, arched and wide behind, and at one end there is a strong claw. When moving, the conch shoves out his foot, sticks this claw into the sand, and uses it to thrust himself forward. He takes a rather uneven course but gets there all the same.

When in a hurry the conch moves in quick, awkward leaps and jumps, its shell flopping from side to side. But it really covers the ground. This claw of his serves also as an operculum, or door, for his shell when he wants to close himself in from his enemies.

72

Conch moving

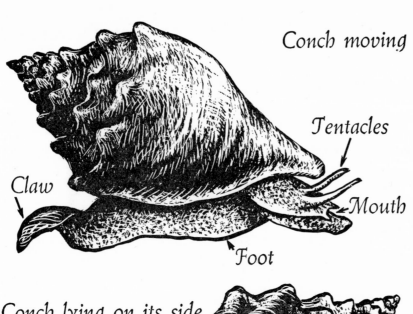

Claw

Tentacles

Mouth

Foot

Conch lying on its side

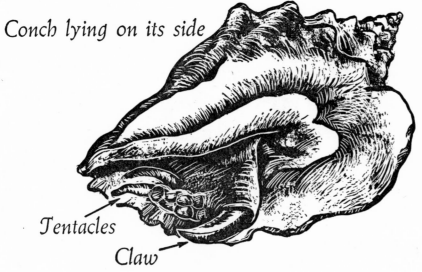

Tentacles

Claw

When young the conch has a very thin shell which is easily pierced by its enemies, such as crabs or fish. So its life, for a while, is not very secure. However, nature seems to have taken care of this to some extent. In some species, the young conch is very similar in shape, color, and markings to another shell, a poisonous one, called the cone shell. Fish, crabs, and other enemies avoid these cone shells because of their poisonous sting. And they let these young conch shells alone too because they look so much like the poisonous cones.

As the conchs grow older, however, their shells get heavy and thick and do not look at all like the little cones. But by that time their big shells keep them fairly safe so they no longer need this camouflage. There is one exception to this. One species that lives in the South Pacific keeps its resem-

Cone shell

Baby conch
shell

blance to the poisonous cone all through its life.

Man is probably the chief enemy of the adult conch. Many are killed, too, by shell animals that are able to drill through the shell of the conch, thick as it is. One enemy of this kind, called the tulip shell, likes to eat these conchs so well that it is called the conch killer.

There are quite a few different kinds of conchs and they all like warmth, so you find them living in tropical waters. The kinds with which we are most familiar are those that live on the Florida coast. One of them, the queen conch, has a big, beautiful pearly shell with polished rosy lips. The pink, outer layer of these lips is sometimes used in

75

making cameos. This conch is the largest mollusk we have that is native to our shores. The shells often weigh as much as five pounds and sometimes grow to be a whole foot long!

Fighting conch

The fighting conch is smaller but very active and is the one seen most often along our Florida beaches.

Conch shells are very abundant in the Bahamas, and in some places they completely cover the ocean floor. They make quite a sight when viewed from the glass-bottom boats. Natives there use them for food. They also make a great deal of money by exporting hundreds of thousands of these shells to Florida. Some of the conchs live to a very great age, losing much of their beauty as they grow older and older.

The conch shell is very lovely and so is highly prized for decorative purposes—the queen conch, especially. You see many of them in Florida homes and yards, bordering gardens, fountains, and paths. They even use them in cemeteries to decorate graves. One species is used so often in this way that it is actually known as the graveyard conch.

Cleaned up and polished, conch shells make lovely souvenirs and very attractive gifts. Many tourists buy them and send them to their friends or bring them home for ornaments. So you can find these souvenir shells in almost all parts of the United States.

77

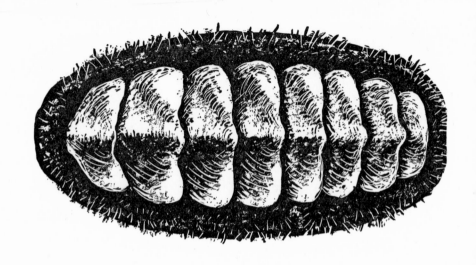

IX THE CHITON HAS EIGHT SHELLS

There are sea animals that have only one shell.
And sea animals that have two shells. And there is
even one strange sea creature that has eight shells
attached to its body!

The chiton it is called (pronounced ki'ton). It's
a mollusk (with its soft body and hard shell) and

yet different from all other mollusks in that its shell is made up of eight sections, or plates.

These eight shell sections are joined together very neatly and firmly, with the bottom of each overlapping the top of the next, like shingles laid on a roof. Coat-of-mail shells they are sometimes called because of this fine hard shell protection. Also sea-cradles because, turned over, they do look like cradles or boats.

The chiton's eight shells are very firmly attached to a tough, leathery girdle, or skin, which often covers them completely, extending out a little beyond the shells and underneath as far as the animal's body. This girdle acts as a sort of multiple hinge, allowing the chiton's body to fasten itself around uneven sections of rock and even curl into a ball when molested.

The chiton's body is rather like that of the limpet. It has a foot and a mantle and a mouth. The chiton likes to live on rocks, too, just as the limpet does. But the chiton is not nearly as lively or active.

With his vacuum disk foot the chiton can fasten himself down even tighter than a limpet. The edges of his leather girdle help protect the vacuum pull of the disk feet, making it easier for him to hang on. Then, too, the jointed shell makes it possible for the chiton to fit into smaller crevices and onto more uneven surfaces. So he can hold tight wherever he is.

Most chitons do not care for the sunlight. They prefer to come out in the darkness, like the owl. So during the day they fasten themselves very firmly, with the suction of their broad feet, onto some rock where the water isn't too deep. And there they like to rest undisturbed.

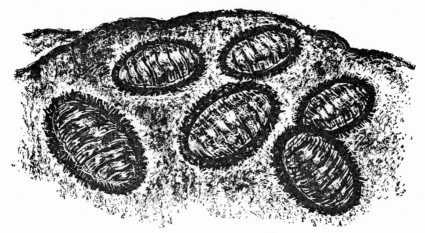

Chitons on rock

When night comes—or sometimes during a dark, foggy day—they make their way slowly, with many others of their kind, to a nearby patch of seaweed. Here they eat their fill of vegetable matter, then go back to the rock before sunup. Chitons are more socially inclined than limpets. Often they pile themselves one on top of another, entirely filling a crack or crevice.

Chitons aren't very easy to see. Most of them

81

are colored on the outside like the rocks on which they live, usually brown, gray, or black. They fasten themselves so firmly to the rock and are so well camouflaged you'd think at first glance they were just something growing there. In many species fine hair or bristles grow out from the leather girdles in such a way as to make them hardly noticeable among the green moss and sea plants on the rock.

If you happen to come across a group of chitons some day at low tide and try to pry one loose from his rock, you will be amazed to see how hard this is to do. If you slip a blunt knife under him quickly, breaking the vacuum, he'll come off in your hand. Then watch the strange way he acts. He'll curl up immediately into a tight round ball. And he will stay that way, too—so tightly wound that it's almost impossible to uncurl him with your

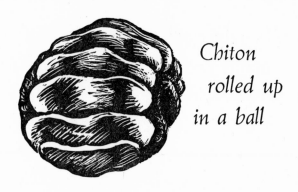

*Chiton
rolled up
in a ball*

hands without breaking some of his muscles or shells.

That is how he protects himself. And it is a good way, too. Because, when he stays all tightly curled up like that, very soon you are apt to get discouraged and toss him back into the water. Which is just what he wants.

Chitons are found on the west coast of the United States, mostly in the warmer waters, although some species can be found as far north as Alaska. They are also found in tropical seas in many other parts of the world. Chitons range in size from small ones two inches long to giant ones as long as eight inches.

Its shells—always eight—are often very beautifully colored. Some have delicate shadings of pink and green; some are black lined and dotted with blue; others are brown or bright orange or turquoise, and some a gay scarlet.

Often along the California beaches you can find separate shells from dead chitons washed up along the shore. Six of these shells are shaped very much like wings and because of this, as well as their pretty colors, they are called butterfly shells. A good name for such lovely shells.

The two end shells are shaped rather like what their name suggests. They are called false-teeth shells.

The best way to find live chitons is to look carefully along the rocks at low tide. To keep a speci-

False-teeth shell

men from curling up, collectors let the chiton fasten itself to a wet wooden slat and then tie it down carefully so it will dry in the proper position.

The beautifully colored separate shells can be found best along the beach after a storm at sea or a very high tide. If you don't have an opportunity to visit the western beaches and to hunt for your own, try trading for one with a shell pal. Or you may have friends in California who can send you some of the lovely sea cradles quite common there.

85

X THE SNAIL IS A LANDLUBBER
COUSIN

All these shell animals we have been talking about live in the sea. But there is a cousin of all these animals, a little creature who belongs to the same family, yet makes his home on land.

You probably have seen one or another of these land relatives, even held one in your hand

and wondered about him. Because he's none other than the familiar snail. He's a mollusk, having a soft body and shell. But since the snail lives on land instead of water like his cousins he has lungs, or respiratory organs, instead of gills. And he is called a land mollusk. Which is rather like the way we speak of our "city cousins" and our "country cousins."

Of course, there are river snails and pond snails as well as sea snails and land snails. But land snails are the ones we are interested in here. And there are a great many different kinds of them.

The land snail gets around on his good strong foot much as some of his sea cousins do. And, though he lives on dry land, he must keep himself moist in order to thrive. So he stays out of the sun as much as he can. He likes to sleep in the daytime and then wake up and get busy at night. And he likes to live in damp and well-watered places.

But sometimes and in some places where snails live—as in southern California—there may be times when even the nights are dry. Or perhaps, as in the sections farther east, the weather is quite cold. Then he just burrows down into the sand or mud for protection, or finds some safe, sheltered spot—under a stone, for instance, or even a leaf.

Once safely hidden away, he slips into his shell and spins a heavy curtain across the entrance. This curtain serves two purposes—it protects him from his enemies, such as birds and glowworms; and it keeps out dry air so his body will stay moist, much as the baker wraps bread in oil paper to protect it from flies and such, and to keep it from drying out.

And so the snail, quietly hidden in his shell, sleeps happily behind his specially woven curtain.

Here he is usually quite safe, and moist and comfy until the rains come again or, in colder climates, until the weather is warmer and more to his liking.

There are all kinds of snails, of course, in all parts of the world. In California many of the shells are brownish in color with darker bands running around the turns of the shells. Washington and Oregon have snails like this but with more beautiful markings. California has another snail, too, shaped differently and almost black in color, which burrows in the ground and stays there all summer waiting for the winter rains.

In the eastern and central states one of the commonest land snails has a thin, transparent shell which is decorated with streaks of reddish brown that zigzag across the whorls.

The streaked mountain snail is found in the Rocky Mountain region. It has two brown bands separated by a white band going around its shell.

Most univalve shells, which include our snails, are "righthanded." This means the opening of their shells is on the right-hand side. There is one land snail, however, that sometimes has its opening on the left-hand side. And these specimens, when found now and then, are very much prized by collectors. Called the European brown snail, it is about one and a half inches in diameter, brownish yellow, with four or five bands of brownish spots and threads of yellow. Native to Europe, where it is used for food, it is common in California and found also around New Orleans, Louisiana, and Charleston, South Carolina.

Land snails of different kinds can be found all over the United States. So no matter where you live you'll probably find at least one kind common to your part of the country. They range in size from tiny ones a tenth of an inch in diameter to larger ones around two and one-half inches or more. Most land snails are vegetarians and feed on green plants and such. A few are carnivorous (meat eating) and feed on other snails and animal matter.

The best place to look for most species is in damp places under decaying logs and leaves and under stones. One of the commonest woodland

species found throughout most of this country is the white-lipped snail. Its shell is about one inch in diameter and a yellowish brown, with sometimes a pinkish hue.

There is one common species that likes open country better than woods. It is found mostly in pastures and open grasslands. It's called the three-toothed snail and is grayish brown, about three-fourths of an inch in diameter.

One species, the Roman snail, is native to Europe but common around New Orleans. It is thought to be quite "intelligent." Its senses of smell, hearing, and sight seem unusually good for a snail. And, like the limpet, it can find its way home after wandering quite far afield for its food. Perhaps it does this by following back along the slimy trail it leaves as it moves.

Cuba has the most interesting snails of all: the

painted snails. They have gorgeously colored shells—yellow circled with bright scarlet; brown with white bands; dark blue with white-edged black bands; salmon red with black and white bands; and so on.

Another strange thing—these Cuban snails live in the trees. No crawling around and burrowing in the ground for them. It's really quite a sight to see these gaily colored snails moving about high up in the trees.

Of course, since the trees in Cuba are pretty colorful too, the snails match their background rather well. They don't stand out quite as much as they would in our trees, for instance. Still it is very startling to see them up there.

Snails and their habits are interesting to study. You might like to keep some in a snailery for a while and watch them. You can make a snailery in a good-sized glass jar if you wish. Just put moist earth or leaf mold in the bottom and use a screened top so they can't crawl out.

Or, if you wish to give them more room to move about in, use a large wooden box. Spread the bottom of the box with moist earth and cover the box with wire to keep the snails in.

Since snails must have moisture to be healthy and happy be sure the earth is always moist. It dries out quickly so keep an eye on it. It's well, too, to keep a small dish of water in one corner.

For food you can give the snail any leaves that you yourself eat. It particularly likes lettuce and cabbage. For furniture you might put in a piece of bark or a board or even a good-sized leaf or two. It likes to have something like that to crawl under when it is ready to rest.

If you would like to raise snails, get them in the

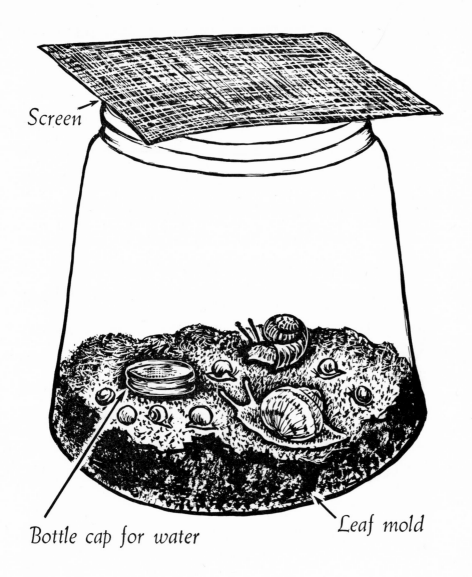

Screen

Bottle cap for water

Leaf mold

springtime when they lay their eggs and before you know it you will have quite a family.

If you wish to go into this snail-raising business in a more efficient way, use a large box and have your earth quite deep—deep enough, in fact, to plant a little fernery or other shade-loving plants in one section. The snails will love this and thrive. Be careful not to let them get out into the garden, however, where they can damage the plants.

Handle the baby snails carefully when they are small. Their shells are so soft and delicate at first it is easy to crush them without meaning to. Better still, do not handle them at all for a while. It will be fun just watching them grow and studying their habits from babyhood until their pretty spiral shells get hard and firm.

XI   SEA URCHINS

You probably have seen food being put through a grinder many a time. Onions, peppers, and tomatoes to make a relish; potatoes and meat for a delicious hash. You even may have done it yourself. But you'd never think of putting sand through that grinder to get something to eat.

There is a little sea animal that grinds up sand to get food however—and inside himself too. It's the green sea urchin. In order to get a meal he swallows a great amount of sand. And he is able, through a sort of grinding, sifting process, to take out all the nourishing bits of food—mostly vegetable matter—from this sand and digest it.

Then he sends the pure sand back out. Only, the sand by now is much finer—just as though it had been put through a grinder. In fact, in some spots where a great many of these sea urchins live close together you actually can see a difference in the texture of the sand, since they had been grinding away at it so busily. It is quite a bit finer than sand anywhere else.

Not all sea urchins get their food this way. The purple sea urchin, for instance, found in large numbers on the Pacific coast, makes his home among rocks. And he gets his food from tiny life living there among the mosses and seaweed.

The sea urchin isn't a mollusk like the other animals you've been reading about. He and the starfish (next chapter) belong to a different family. They are often called Radiates because their mouth is in the center and the other parts of their body radiate out from it.

The sea urchin is completely covered with spines sticking out in all directions. These protect him from his enemies (fish, sea birds, and starfish) and help him to move about. On some of the sea urchins the spines are quite small and fine. On others they are long, thick as lead pencils, and very sharp. If you ever have tried to handle one of these bristling creatures you know why they often are called sea porcupines! These spines are not dangerous, of course, like the porcupine's quills. Though prickly to handle, they can't come off and stick into you like that (except for one kind found on coral reefs whose spines can stick into you and give you a painful sting).

The sea urchin can move each one of these spines separately on its "ball and socket" joint much as we can move one of our arms and legs when we do so without bending it. The sea urchin also has many tube feet with suckers on the end. These stick out from among the spines and help him get about.

By fastening and unfastening these suckers the animal is able to climb over rocks quite steep. These tube feet also help to serve as breathing organs, although most species have gills for breathing as well.

The sea urchin's mouth, as we've mentioned, is in the middle of its body. And it has a remarkable set of jaws with five long projecting teeth. This set of jaws is called Aristotle's lantern be-

Sea urchins among the rocks at low tide

cause it is shaped like this lantern—a rather strange thing to find in a sea creature like this. These teeth are very useful to him, however, in chewing his food and in chiseling out a cozy nook. Since he lives mostly among rocks where the waves are quite rough, he must find some way to make himself safe, to more or less dig himself in. This he does with his five strong teeth and strong pointed spines. This sounds a little

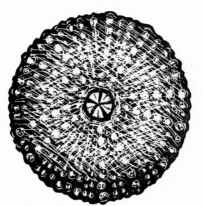

Aristotle's lantern

Urchin without spines, showing tips of teeth

easier than using a shell and foot as the piddock has to do. But it's not too easy at that.

He first finds a small depression on a rock. Then he sets to work and by keeping constantly in motion, scraping with tooth and spine, he will finally have a little place hollowed out, big enough so that at least the bottom half of his body can get wedged in. And here he can stay, quite safely, no matter how rough the waves. Sometimes, when the hole is small and he keeps growing, he gets wedged in for good. He is there for the rest of his life.

But it does not bother him. He seems perfectly content to be there. Nor does it bother him if he wears down his teeth in digging this nest. Because very soon he can grow them all out again to the proper length.

Both the purple and the green sea urchins are

103

found quite abundantly along the Pacific coast. The green sea urchin is also found on the Atlantic coast as far south as New Jersey. Sea urchins usually are about two inches across but one species of the Pacific coast, found in deeper tide pools, grows sometimes as big as eight inches across.

The best time to look for sea urchins is after a storm at sea. Many empty skeletons often are found tossed up on the beach with their spines worn off. These are very interesting because they show all their pretty markings. And if you are lucky, the strange jaws and teeth may still be inside. Sometimes you can find sea urchins on the beach with their spines still on. But they probably will be dead since these animals can't live long out of water.

Low tide is the best time to find live specimens. Sometimes in the tide pools whole colonies will fill the nooks and crannies of the rocks as far as your eye can see. The purple sea urchins of the Pacific coast can often be found this way and it's a lovely, colorful sight to see.

Many authorities feel that the sea urchin's covering is not really a shell because of the way its body is formed. They prefer to call it a test, which means "thin protective covering."

There is a relative of the sea urchin that is very interesting, too. It is called the sand dollar. It's a round, flat disk about three inches across and does, sometimes, resemble a silver dollar.

This sea animal has its mouth in the center of its body, has tiny tube feet and small spines. The spines of the sand dollar are fine and short and silky, however. They feel more like velvety hairs than spines. Sometimes you can find sand dollars

105

Sand dollar without spines

Sand dollar, showing spines

washed up on the beach with these spines still on. They'll probably be dead or dying, since sand dollars can't live long out of water either. More often you'll find them after they have been dead for some time, with their spines worn off from the friction of the sea and sand. It is then that they look somewhat like silver dollars: round and with a smooth, bleached, whitish surface. And interesting markings in the center can clearly be seen—pretty designs that look like petals of a flower.

106

The sand dollar lives under water, just under the sand or lying on top of it. He can move about slowly on his short spines and tube feet. And he eats tiny bits of vegetable matter.

When alive the sand dollar is dark brown or purplish at first but later takes on a greenish tint. It is said that fishermen used to grind the spines and skin of the sand dollar to make an indelible ink.

Sand dollars can be found on both the Atlantic and Pacific coasts: on the Atlantic as far south as New Jersey; on the Pacific from Alaska down to Lower California. Many sea urchins and sand dollars live as long as ten years, sometimes longer.

You'll enjoy finding these interesting sea animals and studying their structure and markings, or trading for them if you can't visit the beaches where they are found.

107

XII THE STARFISH

When we eat, we chew and swallow our food and send it down to our stomach. But not so the starfish. Strange as it may seem he sends his stomach out after the food.

Since the starfish has no teeth, he can't chew and swallow his food. But he does have strong

108

tube feet covered with small sucking disks. These make his grip very powerful—as you know if you've ever tried to pull a starfish off a rock to which he is attached. If you pick him up he'll probably come, rock and all. Even though the weight of the rock is considerable he won't let it drop.

When the starfish gets hungry he goes gliding over the rocks on his tube feet looking for dinner. He likes to eat clams, mussels, oysters, and the like, as well as we enjoy chicken or steak. But they are all shell animals, and bivalves, with the ability to close up very tightly when danger is near. And the starfish has no hard jaws to crack open these shells to get at the food inside. Nor can he pick up a closed shell in his bill, as does the sea gull, for instance, fly high in the air, and drop it down against the rocks to smash it open.

But the starfish does have those strong tube feet and he uses them very expertly. He grabs a mussel shell, let us say, and holds on tightly with those sucking disks on his feet. Then he humps up his body in a way that enables his strong tube feet to pull at the closed shells of the mussel.

Nothing happens at first—often for quite a while—because the mussel is strong, too, and can hold the two parts of his shell closed very tightly—as you know if you've ever tried to force one open. In fact, often the animal the starfish goes after is even stronger than he is himself. But the starfish always wins because he can last longer. Very patiently, sometimes for hours on end, he just stays there, humped over the shell, quietly pulling. Finally the victim can't stand the strain any longer. He has to relax and let his shell open up.

Starfish opening mussel shell

Then the starfish sends his stomach right out through his mouth. The stomach just seems to surround the food and digest it then and there. After he has eaten his dinner he tucks his stomach back in and goes slowly along over the rocks looking for another choice morsel.

There are members of the starfish family that can't break open shells like that because they haven't the helpful suckers on their feet. So these go after the smaller shell animals and eat them, shell and all. Their stomach digests the meat and sends out the empty shells later.

The starfish belongs to the same family as the sea urchin and sand dollar. His mouth, too, is in the center of his body and he has a number of sections or points reaching out like points of a star.

You usually think of starfish as having five

points—and many of them do. But some have six points, others eight, ten, fifteen—even twenty. And some have only one.

Starfish are tricky too. One kind will just drop off an arm or point if you try to pick it up that way. And another member of this family seems to like to drop off an arm now and then just for something to do. Maybe he gets tired of having the same old arms, or rays, as they are also called. Perhaps he craves to have something new as we

113

like to get a new coat or shoes. Because that is just what he does—he grows a brand new one to take its place.

And still more wonderful yet, the arm or ray that the starfish dropped off has the power to grow a whole new body—a central part or disk, as it is called, and a complete set of rays—so that after a while he becomes a perfect, whole star-fish too!

Starfish have tiny eyespots at the end of each ray but they aren't very effective as eyes. They can tell light from dark but that's about all. There's a tiny feeler also at the end of each ray which seems to be able to smell out its food and direct the starfish in the proper direction.

Starfish live ten years or longer and are found in both deep or shallow water in every ocean in the world. So, of course, they are on both our

Eye spot

Atlantic and Pacific coasts. They vary in size from tiny ones to large creatures over two feet across.

Starfish are beautifully colored, too—yellow, orange, brown, purple, bright red, green, and blue. Some are mottled, some two-toned with shadings of different colors. One kind found in southern California is a dark brown and is sometimes called the snake skin. It has a small disk and long, thin, wriggly arms covered with a sort of scaly, snakelike skin. It is also called brittle star, because it can drop off an arm easily if it is picked up or touched.

Another very odd species, about a foot in

115

Basket starfish

diameter, is called the basket starfish. It has five main points but each point branches and re-branches, on and on, into a total of hundreds of wriggling arms. These arms serve as a handy basket or net in which to catch its food—small fish as they swim by.

Starfish like to crawl about on the bottom of

the sea on the sand, mud, or over the rocks. They are quite active when the tide is high. At low tide they hide beneath ledges and rocks, so this is the best time to look for them.

Sometimes hundreds of starfish, of all sizes, shapes, and colors, can be seen hiding in the crevices and depressions of the rocks and in the tide pools, making a beautifully colored picture. You won't often be lucky enough to find them that way. There probably will be just a few hidden here and there among the rocks. But you can see them if you look for them. And you may come across dead specimens too, washed up on the beach after a storm.

Certainly they are interesting sea creatures and fun to find.

117

XIII NICKNAMES ON THE SAND

If you should hear someone say: "I had a fine walk along the beach today. I found a coffee bean, a slipper, and a horn"—would you wonder what he was talking about?

A coffee bean, a slipper, and a horn! On the beach? What a strange collection of things to be so pleased about.

They are all sea shells. And the person talking about them would probably be a conchologist (pronounced kŏng-kŏl′ōō-jĭst), or shell collector.

Shells need not be called by their long names because most of them have easy nicknames. Just as we call our friends by special names—a tall

118

boy, Slim; a red-haired fellow, Red—so shells are given special names that have to do with the way they look.

The coffee bean is called that because it looks quite a bit like a coffee bean. It is flat on one side, round on the other, and is like a coffee bean in size and color.

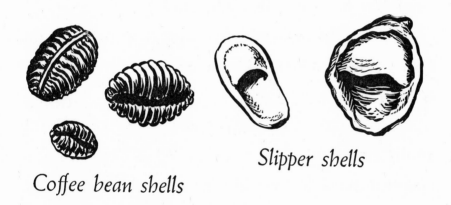

Slipper shells

Coffee bean shells

The slipper shell looks like a tiny little slipper, or mule. It is broad and rounded and has a little open half section on top—if your foot were small

Horn shells

enough you could slip it right in! As you can see by the picture.

And the horn, though small, is long and narrow with a tiny hole at the top almost inviting you to give it a "toot."

You've already read about the sand dollar.

Dunce cap limpet

Wavy top shell

Round and flat, when it's bleached white on the sands it looks quite like a silver dollar.

There are some shells shaped just like a little dunce cap and these are called dunce cap limpets. They belong to the limpet family we read about earlier. Another shell of the same family has a little opening in the top like a keyhole—they are called keyhole limpets. Look back to the picture illustrating the limpet story and see if you can pick out the keyhole limpets in the group shown there. There's a volcano limpet too. It is called this because the fiery red stripes running down its sides look like a lava flow.

Then there's the turban shell, shaped like a turban or a head covering, and the wavy-top shell with its wavy edges. The bleeding tooth shell is well named, too. You probably can tell from the picture. It has two little teeth stained

Bleeding-tooth shell   *Sundial shell*

with a yellowish bloody color. And the sundial shell and the worm shell also look like their names.

Bubble shells are well named, they are so thin

Worm shell

and fragile. They must be handled with special care if you want them to remain whole in your collection.

Bubble shells

Jingle shells

Perhaps you know about jingle shells and have picked them up. They are also called potato chips or devil's toenails. They are found on both the

123

Atlantic and the Pacific coasts, but are more common along the Atlantic. Small and dainty with pretty colors of yellow, pink, or silver, they clink musically in your hands when you shake them.

There are a great many others, of course. For instance, there are the ladder shells, the cup and saucer limpets, the frog shells, and the umbrella shells; the tooth shells, wing shells, and the star shells. Looking at them you probably can see why they were named as they were.

Shells have nicknames just as people have. And it is well that they do. Certainly we shell collectors find it easier to say:

"I found a bubble shell today," than

"I found a *Hamines virescens* today." Or even

"Look! there's a *Bulla gouldiana!*"

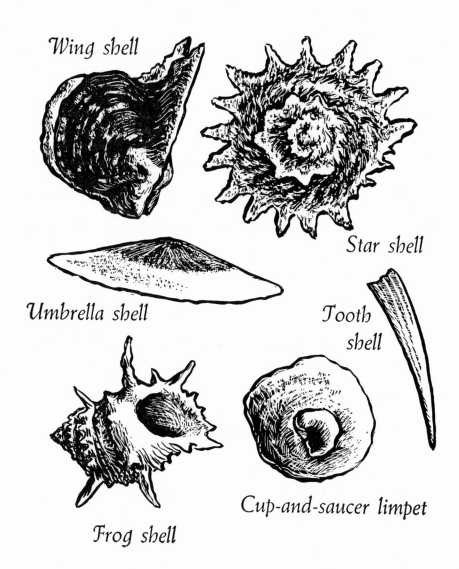

Wing shell

Star shell

Umbrella shell

Tooth shell

Frog shell

Cup-and-saucer limpet

XIV   TREAT 'EM RIGHT

Hunting for shells is mighty fascinating—as you know if you've ever done it. There are so many different kinds to be found in so many different places one should really be always on the alert.

Tide pools are wonderful spots to visit. They

are like little aquariums among the rocks, filled with colorful, interesting sea life. It is amazing the variety of shells and sea animals that are found there. You can have a wonderful time just watching the activity that is constantly going on, even if you're not out to collect shells. And if you are, you'll want to search these pools with especial care.

Also you will want to look along the rocks and ledges that stretch above the water when the tide is low—and under the rocks, if they're not too large to turn over. You may find choice specimens there. But be sure to turn the rock back again or the sea life left exposed will die.

And go adequately prepared. Wear tennis shoes on your feet or thick soled shoes so you won't get cut by sharp rocks or shells. Take some sacks along—orange net bags are good—for the

larger shells you'll find. And small boxes or bottles for the smaller, fragile shells. And a pail filled with sea water in which to drop shells that need this attention. A thin-bladed knife or spatula is necessary if you want to get live limpets or chitons from the rocks.

To find a good variety of shells it is wise to visit as many different types of places where they might be as you possibly can. And as many different times as possible. Some shells are found best at low tide. Others may be more easily secured when the tide is high. One day the beaches or rocks might be filled with a wonderful variety and the very next day scarcely any at all may be in view. The kind and number of shells to be found may vary with the weather, the season of the year, tide conditions, and many things. So it's best to be always on the alert and to take advantage of every chance you have to add to your collection.

When shell hunting remember to look along wooden or concrete supports under old docks. Many kinds of shell animals are often hidden there. Sand bars, too, are usually most rewarding. And mud flats are worth searching—for the beautiful angel's wings, if nothing else.

Walk very carefully along the sand bars and mud flats when you're looking for shells. Most bivalves hidden there are very sensitive to vibra-

tions. They will hear you coming, close up tight, and dig deep to get out of the way. If you keep a watchful eye out as you walk along you may see small sprays of water spurting up from tiny holes in the sand. This is caused when the bivalve shoots out the water inside its shell in order to close it, and pull itself down deeper into its burrow.

If you dig down, not right on the hole but just to one side, you'll probably find the sea animal that is hiding there. If you're after angel's wings, dig deeply—their burrows sometimes reach down two feet or more. Angel's wings are very

130

fragile. They even break their own shells sometimes if they are too suddenly startled and clamp
the shells together too tightly. When you find
one put it quickly and carefully into a pail of sea
water so its fright won't cause it to break its shell.

Empty shells tossed up on the beach by the
waves are the easiest of all to find. Sometimes
they are still whole and pretty, especially if you
hunt for them among seaweed freshly washed in.
Shells often become caught in this seaweed and
are protected from the banging around by the
waves they otherwise would get.

Often, however, shells tossed up on the beach
are damaged or worn, the pretty polish rubbed
off. If you find a new shell this way, one you
haven't found before, keep it, of course, until
you can find a better one.

True conchologists say if you really want

131

bright, whole specimens in your collection it is better to get them with the animals still alive inside. It's more trouble, of course, but your collection will have more value—if that interests you.

When you get your shells home, don't just dump them in a box and forget them. The empty shells that were picked up on the beach won't need so much attention. Just wash them carefully and lay them out to dry in the shade.

Shells with the animals still in them will need special care. Small univalve shells are hardest to clean. So it is best to let them soak for a few days in a 4 per cent solution of formaldehyde (one part formaldehyde to nine parts water). This will kill any odor of decay so you won't have to worry about digging the tiny animal out. Starfish can be treated this way, too. If you tie them

132

down they will dry in a more natural position.

Larger univalves and the bivalves should be placed in a basin of fresh water and put on the stove over a low heat. After the water has come slowly to a boil, take the basin off and let the water cool. Bivalve shells will have opened and you can clean the animal out quite easily. Any parts that stick to the shell can be carefully scraped with a blunt knife.

Some univalves will clean easily. But for others you will need a crochet hook or hooked wire to insert into the spiral opening and draw out the animal inside. Clean the outside of the shells carefully and put them out in the shade to dry.

If you want to be really professional you should identify and label your shells. If you aren't sure what type of shell each one is, consult the reference books on the subject that are in your library. Then write in its name, the scientific as well as the nickname, if you have been able to find both of them. Underneath you can write where you found it, when, and by whom it was found.

Select the best specimens you have of each kind and file them away with these proper identifications. If you have any empty drawers, you can put in partitions and keep your shells in

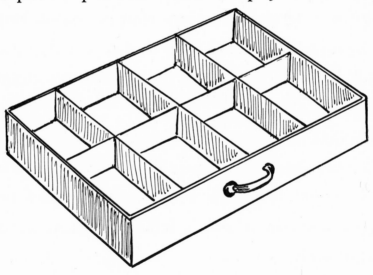

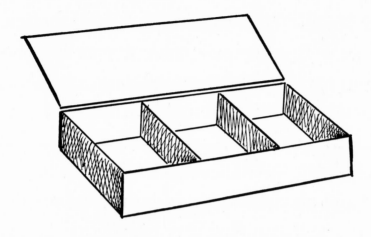

these. Small shells had better go in boxes of some sort for added protection. Empty match boxes are good for this. And cigar boxes are often used. Stick gummed labels on the outside to identify each box of shells.

If you know someone who works in a business office get him to save empty metal typewriter ribbon boxes. These are fine for filing away your special specimens with a little identification card underneath.

135

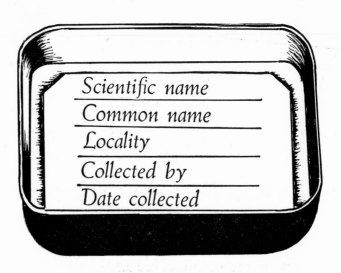

One good way to store these typewriter ribbon boxes of shells is to use a good, deep cardboard box (see picture). From extra cardboard cut four or five strips of a size to fit into the box like shelves. Run string through holes at each end to make handles. Then you can arrange your shells, all snug in their little typewriter ribbon boxes, along each cardboard strip and lift the whole thing in and out with ease. And you can

136

file several layers away, on top of one another, without hurting any of the shells.

There are many ways to care for your shells. If you have room for a cabinet and can arrange your best ones in it where they can be seen, but protected by glass from dust and damage,

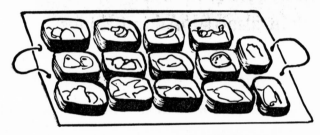

Cardboard tray

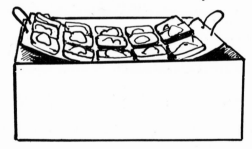

Box with tray

you can have some fine displays. But do take care of them.

And if you have too many of one kind, don't throw them away. Start trading with other shell collectors. They might want your extras very much and have some kind to give that you haven't been able to find.

You might also try making things with your extra shells. One boy bought some modeling clay and, using this with his extra shells, made all kinds of animals and figures which he sold for fifteen cents each. Ordinary pipe cleaners are handy, too, to use with your shells in making things. So are small feathers, bits of plastic, felt, and the like.

Notice some of the things in the picture that were made with shells. Use your imagination and see what interesting things you can do.

138

There are so many kinds of shells all over the world it would be pretty hard to try to include them all in your collection. A good way to start is to try to get a good variety of the kind of shells

found in your own locality, if you live near the coast; or the ones found where you visit if you sometimes get to the beaches.

If you live inland, you might get a good start by buying a small beginning collection. Watch the advertisements in the hobby magazines and you might have a chance to make a good deal with someone who is selling his. If you collect other things, such as stamps or rocks, often you can trade some of these for shells. Let your friends and relatives know you are interested in shells and they'll send or bring you choice specimens when they travel about. Maybe you'll get to like one special kind or species of shell so well you'll want to collect all sorts that come under this general family heading. Some people just collect miniatures—all the tiny shells they can find.

Or you might correspond with a pen pal or two.

Listed in the back of this book are the names and addresses of the shell clubs now active in this country. The list was compiled by Dr. Howard R. Hill of the Los Angeles Museum. The clubs will give you the names of pen pals—shell collectors in their vicinity who might be interested in corresponding with you and doing some trading.

Anyway, whatever you decide to do, you're sure to have fun with your shells. Good luck and good hunting!

SHELL CLUBS IN THE UNITED STATES

The Conchological Club of Southern California
Los Angeles County Museum, Exposition Park,
Los Angeles 7, California

The Long Beach Shell Club
Main Library, Pacific and Ocean Avenues, Long Beach,
California

Northern California Malacozoological Club
1048 Monterey Avenue, Berkeley 7, California

Clench Conchological Club
Worcester Natural History Museum, Worcester, Massachusetts

142

New York Shell Club

>American Museum of Natural History, Central Park West and 79th Street, New York 24, New York

St. Petersburg Shell Club

>Saint Petersburg, Florida

Conchological Section

>Buffalo Museum of Natural History, Buffalo, New York

Boston Malacological Club

>Massachusetts Audubon Society Library, Boston, Massachusetts

BOOKS ABOUT SEA SHELLS

Shells and seashore life are so interesting you probably will want to learn more about them. These are some of the books that should be helpful to you:

Arnold, A. F. *Sea Beach at Ebb Tide*. New York: Appleton-Century-Crofts, 1901.

Buchsbaum, Ralph. *Animals without Backbones*. Chicago: University of Chicago Press, 1940.

Burgess, T. W. *The Burgess Sea-Shore Book for Children*. Boston: Little, Brown, and Company, 1931.

Butler, E. L. *Along the Shore*. New York: The John Day Company, 1930.

Crowder, W. *Between the Tides*. New York: Dodd, Mead and Company, 1931.

Crowder, W. *Dwellers of the Sea and Shore*. New York: The Macmillan Company, 1935.

Gaylord, I. N. *Little Sea Folk*. Boston: Little, Brown and Company, 1930.

Hausman, Leon A. *Beginner's Guide to Seashore Life*. New York: G. P. Putnam's Sons, 1949.

Henderson, Daniel. *Children of the Tide.* New York: D. Appleton and Company, 1931.

Huey, E. G. *A Child's Study of the Animal World.* New York: Reynal and Hitchcock, 1935.

Johnson, M. E., and Snook, H. J. *Seashore Animals of the Pacific Coast.* New York: The Macmillan Company, 1927.

Keep, J. *West Coast Shells.* Stanford, Calif.: Stanford University Press, 1935.

Morris, P. A. *A Field Guide to the Shells (of Our Atlantic and Gulf Coasts).* Boston: Houghton Mifflin Company, 1947.

Pratt, H. S. *Manual of the Common Invertebrate Animals.* Philadelphia: P. Blackiston's Son and Company, 1935.

Ricketts, E. F., and Calvin, J. *Between Pacific Tides.* Stanford, Calif.: Stanford University Press, 1939.

Rogers, Julia Ellen. *The Shell Book.* New York: Doubleday and Company, 1939.

Verrill, A. Hyatt. *Shell Collector's Handbook.* New York: G. P. Putnam's Sons, 1950.

Wells, Harrington. *Seashore Life.* San Francisco, Calif.: Harr Wagner Publishing Company, 1937.

145

INDEX

149

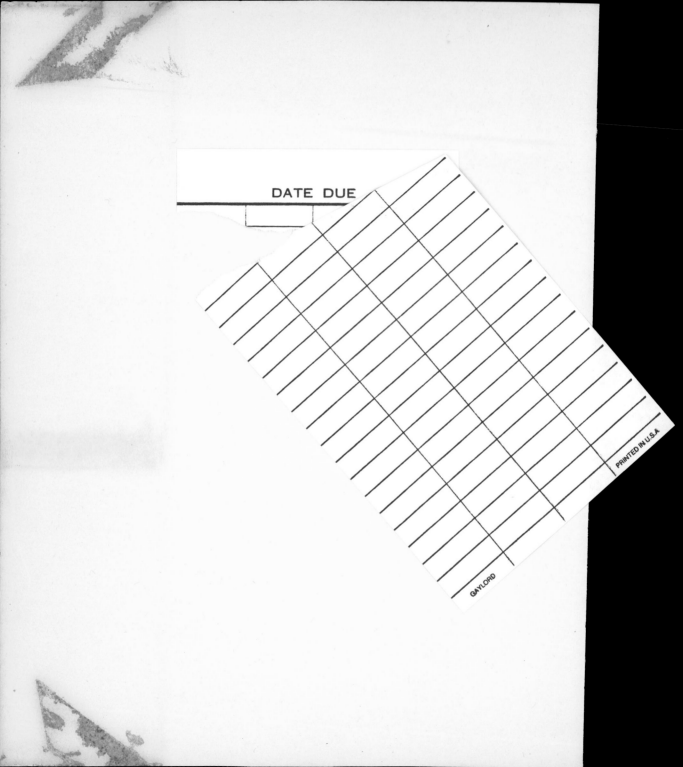

DATE DUE

GAYLORD

PRINTED IN U.S.A